ROCKS AND FISTS:
DECIMATING THE 141ST NVA REGIMENT

BY
T.A. WILLIAMSON

࿎

ILLUSTRATIONS BY
DAVID BRUNEAU

ISBN–13: 978-1517160913
ISBN–10: 151716091X

Dedication

This book is dedicated to fallen Marines and Sailors of the 3rd Battalion, 7th Marines, during Tet 1969.

Table of Contents

Preface

One of the legacies of the Vietnam War is the notion held by some that the military was outmatched strategically on the ground by the wily Viet Cong and North Vietnamese Army. It is true that American might and technological superiority did not carry the day in the end, but there is little doubt that U.S. Forces did prevail time and time again on the battlefield.

Some of the U.S. grand strategies, such as McNamara's ill-conceived and resource-wasting barrier, were dismal failures, but the "grunt" units closest to the combat did employ sophisticated tactics and technology that were successful against their determined enemy. The efforts of the 3rd Battalion, 7th Marines, in the Hieu Duc District in early 1969 is one such example.

This work was more than 18 months in the making, primarily because of the difficulty of tracking down the participants who fought with the battalion during Tet 1969, a far lesser known series of battles than the infamous Tet 1968. After 45 years, some memories are remarkable but others are at best sketchy.

Some of the gaps were hard to fill and the author accepts responsibility for any errors or omissions that resulted. I am especially grateful to the former Marines who did open up on sometimes painful memories to tell their story. Although a former platoon commander with Mike Company, one of the units in the battle, the author was serving in another capacity with the battalion at the time.

The account of the U.S. Marines during the war is fairly well documented in the *Marines in Vietnam* series of the U.S. Government Printing Office and there are a few primary sources on the battalion's role during the February battle, including then-Captain Paul K. Van Riper's article in the *Marine Corps Gazette* and Merrill Bartlett's article in the same publication. Especially useful were the USMC command chronologies that lay out in great detail the monthly operations of the battalion units throughout the division.

The photos are from my private collection, except for those showing scenes from Mike's engagement, which are courtesy of Gary Walker.

Finally, you are encouraged to read the two sidebars in the Addendum which tells the fascinating back story of Medal of Honor recipient Lester Weber and an account of the battalion's nemesis, the 141st NVA Regiment and its hard-core Communist leader.

Introduction

Vietnam was a war of footnotes for many who fought there, devoid of famous battles or well-known campaigns. But the combat that was the everyday lot of the Marine infantryman could be just as deadly and intense.

So it was for the 3rd Battalion, 7th Marines (3/7) in the days preceding and including little Tet or post-Tet[1] in early 1969. After five days of close-quarters fighting with rifle butts, CS (tear) gas and "mostly rocks and fists," as one zealous Marine described it, the 141st Regiment of the Peoples' Army of Vietnam—commonly called the North Vietnamese Army (NVA)—was decimated. There were 137 enemy dead and the NVA's second major attack on Da Nang was crushed.

The Communists had been consumed with controlling the Republic of (South) Vietnam's second largest urban area from the earliest days of the conflict when the country was divided in 1954 as a result of the Geneva Convention. Marines in the southern portion of I Corps (the northernmost of the four military tactical zones of South Vietnam) had been clashing with Communist forces since their unopposed landings in 1965 on the beaches of Da Nang.

---

1. Some of the name confusion may be caused by timing in that it was launched on February 23 following the Vietnamese New Year on February 16, but within the seven-day celebration of Tet. Compounding the issue is the fact that North Vietnam and South Vietnam used slightly differing calendars. Indeed, for the attack during Tet 1968, NVA units in the 5th Military Region nearest North Vietnam launched their attacks on January 29 and units in the south attacked the night of January 30.

Until early December 1968, 3/7 operated in the flat terrain south of Route 4 primarily in "Dodge City,"[2] so-called because there was always a shootout, and parts of the adjacent "Arizona Territory." Marine companies and battalions often conducted large-scale operations against similarly sized enemy units in clashes akin to conventional warfare. It was such a contentious region that certain areas had been cleared of inhabitants to create "free fire" zones where artillery and air strikes could be called at will without clearance from local Vietnamese authorities. Areas around An Hoa, and Go Noi Island were particularly infested with NVA.

In one savage campaign launched on November 20, 1968, by seven battalions under control of the 1st Marine Regiment, more than 1,000 NVA were killed in fighting some senior Marines called the fiercest they had ever seen.

Maj. Gen. Carl A. Youngdale, Deputy Commanding General of the III Marine Amphibious Force, said the results of the campaign, designated Operation Meade River, should be the end of "the enemy's stranglehold on the Dodge City area." The fighting ended December 9, but by the end of the month, the NVA were back and once again owned the area of the campaign, just a short walk of two or three miles south from the 7th Marine Regiment headquarters on Hill 55 (so named for its height in meters).

The Hieu Duc District, immediately south of Da Nang, had long been a hotbed of enemy activity when 3/7 moved north to assume tactical responsibility for the area. Dotted with hamlets, rice paddies and dense tree lines, the district had a well-developed Viet Cong (VC) infrastructure with friendly villagers and ample rice resources for the NVA

---

2. The geographic area of Dodge City has been defined in differing ways, but most agree it was about 10 miles south of Da Nang. Generally it was bordered on the north by the La Tho River and on the south by the Ky Lam River. The east boundary was Route 1 and on the west it was the rivers of Vi Gia and Al Nghia, roughly a 28- to-30-square-mile area. The land was very fertile and the Vietnamese would confine their villages to small enclaves of bamboo and thorn hedges, which could be fortified as natural defensive positions with commanding clear fields of fire across the often arid rice paddies. It was festooned with enemy caves, bunkers and tunnels and crisscrossed with rivers and streams that became flooded during the Monsoons.

units traveling from their sanctuaries in the Que Son[3] Mountains east and north through the lowlands toward Da Nang. The traffic was heavy as enemy units brought in 122 millimeter (mm) and 140 mm rockets or small arms to store, carrying rice on the return trip to their enclaves in the mountains

From combat bases strung along Route 504, the north-south macadam highway bordering the low foothills of Charlie Ridge to the west, the Marines' mission was to interdict the NVA. Unlike the battalion's previous Tactical Area of Responsibility (TAOR), the war here was largely waged with small units—squads and fire teams—and it was the Marines who owned the territory. The units became intensely familiar with the terrain, even more than their enemy. Of course, the VC knew the area but by 1969, their northern cousins were doing the bulk of the fighting.

Stopping rocket attacks had been job one for the Marines defending Da Nang from the earliest days of the war. In the southern I Corps, the enemy didn't have artillery but did use long-range Soviet- or Chinese-made rockets, using a solid-propellant delivery system. They could launch the rockets from tripods with aiming devices or from dirt ramps hastily built by small NVA or VC teams on the relatively flat land of the Hieu Duc District.

The rockets often were fired so hastily as the enemy evaded Marine patrols that they were sometimes no more accurate than a kid's bottle rocket. Nonetheless, with a range of more than seven miles and up to three pounds of TNT, they could be effective, even if only as a psychological weapon. Because of the vastness of the airfield and the rest of the Da Nang complex "a complete miss was impossible," noted Maj. Gen. Ormond R. Simpson, commanding officer of the 1st Division, which conducted 500 or more daily patrols in 1969 to stop the rockets and disrupt NVA infiltration routes.

---

3. The mountains were part of the Annamite Range of eastern Indochina, which roughly separate Laos and Vietnam and run parallel to the coast. The war was defined by this geography and NVA attempts to move from north via the Ho Chi Minh Trail via Laos through the mountains in an effort to control the fertile lowlands and urban centers. The hills of "Charlie Ridge" was on the eastern side of the mountain chain and was part of 3/7's TAOR.

When the 3rd battalion, 7th Marines took over the district, rocket attacks were a regular, sometimes daily occurrence. Col. Herbert L. Beckington, 3/7's regimental commander, hoped that a new battalion with a different set of eyes might find some novel solutions to the ubiquitous rocket attacks on Da Nang, noted Lt. Gen. Paul K. Van Riper, the company commander of Mike (M) Company in 1969. As a result, 1st Battalion, 7th Marines swapped TAORs with 3/7 and assumed its responsibility for operations in the Dodge City area and environs south of Hill 55.

1
Tightening the Rocket Belt

Led by Lt. Col. Francis X. Quinn, a bulldog of a Marine who earned a Silver Star as a platoon commander in Korea, the battalion placed Mike (M), Lima (L), and India (I) companies on Hill 10, an ameba of scrapped brown earth about six miles southwest of the Da Nang Airfield. Mike patrolled the area east of the battalion headquarters toward the village of Bo Ban, a village within a salient formed by the Song (river) Tuy Loan. The company was also tasked with manning "Mike Tower" just south of Hill 10, which provided a commanding view of the surrounding rice paddies and hills.

Hill 10, Headquarters of 3rd Battalion, 7th Marines
Quang Nam Province, Republic of South Vietnam

Lima was given the area west and north into the low foothills of Charlie Ridge, including the An Tan Ridge, the site of fierce fighting during Tet 1969. India had responsibility for security at the Cobb Bridge on Route 504, which crossed the Song Tuy Loan, patrolling the La Chau's[4] just east of Hill 41 and "tugboat," a platoon-sized base reached by boat from the bridge. Kilo (K), the fourth infantry company in 3/7, operated from Hill 41, near Route 504, about two miles south of Hill 10.

Quinn, who later retired as a major general, and his company commanders realized that concentrated patrolling and sophisticated surveillance, coupled with search and cordon operations, presented the best opportunity to keep the NVA off-balance and break up the VC infrastructure. Standard Marine operating procedure some might say, but for the 3/7 grunts, it was unlike anything they had experienced. Just one company, Mike, carried out 750 fire team and squad[5] ambushes .

"We were working the area east and south of Hill 41, ambush after ambush. It was never-ending," noted John F. Bender, third platoon commander in Mike's sister company, Kilo. A squad leader with Kilo's first platoon, Jim Berg, added that "there was so little connection with the platoons. We were all doing our thing with ambushes and patrols and they were doing theirs. It really was just small bands of squads."

"We learned that the NVA did not know the area and they were led by VC guides," noted Col. Fred T. Fagan, then-commanding officer of Kilo Company, who shared his experiences in a 1970 article in the Marine Corps Gazette. "If you looked at the maps, it was pretty clear that you know within a 100-meter (yard) area where they were infiltrating (and) the trails they would follow," added Van Riper. "Rockets also

---

4. The names of villages on military maps, generally remakes of French maps, often reflect a number of hamlets clustered together bearing the same name; however sometimes different hamlets will also bear a number designation. In this case, there were four La Chaus numbered 1–4.

5. In 1969 a rifle platoon was based on the standard military triad system consisting of three squads, with three fire teams each. Its Table of Organization called for about 45 men but during Vietnam it was rarely that because of casualties and rotation. An infantry battalion was comprised of four infantry companies, with three rifle platoons each, along with a weapons platoon for crew-served weapons, such as mortars and machine guns

could not be fired from a wet rice paddy, nor could they be fired from underneath any sort of cover, such as trees. It had to be an open area 20-by-20 meters," further limiting enemy options.

"As (we) became more familiar with the terrain, civilians and the enemy, we began to add new methods and techniques designed to keep the enemy off balance and to increase our control over him and his movements," said Fagan, a Naval Academy graduate who earned a reputation among his peers as an aggressive commanding officer.

Fagan explained one of the changes his company instituted. "Ordinarily, all ambushes would break around 0300 or 0400 (3 a.m. or 4 a.m.) and (Marines) would establish a physical cordon around a small hamlet. At first light, a search would be conducted," seeking evidence of the enemy's presence.

In addition to the just-in-time cordon operations, companies conducted more thoroughly planned searches, sometimes employing the Vietnamese National Police Field Force. The police were so well-integrated with the Marines of Mike Company that they even shared sleeping arrangements, said Van Riper, who had served as an advisor to the Vietnamese Marines during his first Vietnam tour.

Savvy small unit leaders were integral to the success of the sophisticated infantry tactics, Fagan noted. Squad and fire team leaders called in supporting arms, coordinated air attacks and read maps "with a coolness

© David Bruneau

3

and efficiency that rivaled the work of company and platoon commanders on my first tour," he said.

Typical of this professionalism was an ambush on February 8, 1969. A squad leader from Mike's second platoon waited patiently for five NVA to move into an ambush kill zone before springing the trap and then calling in pre-arranged blocking fires. Marines dispatched any NVA still alive within minutes with grenades and small arms fire.

"Waiting until morning to sweep a killing zone will result in nothing," Fagan pointed out. "Get out there immediately and aggressively – if you want bodies, prisoners, weapons and documents."

So it went every night, often accompanied by slowly oscillating parachute flares, raising and lowering the curtain of darkness as their amber light reflected in the silvery water of the rice paddies around the battalion headquarters on Hill 10.

The constant illumination was not by happenstance. Van Riper,[6] who earned the reputation as an outside-the-box officer during his career, understood that it would take creative solutions to stop rocket attacks and the NVA resupply effort. Early in 1969, he assembled his platoon commanders and representatives of supporting arms units for a brainstorming session.

In an attempt to add some humor to the situation, one of the officers said, " Skipper, if we had 24 hours daylight, we wouldn't have this problem, would we?" That piqued the interest of 1st Lt. Gene Gray, an artillery forward observer with a penchant for science.

---

6. Lt. Gen. Van Riper was a former enlisted Marine who retired 1997 as the commanding general of the Marine Corps Combat Development Command, which is responsible for training and education functions of the Corps and includes the war-fighting laboratory. He also served as the first president of the Marine Corps University, an accredited higher education institution. Called a "master of military grand strategy" by the Foreign Policy Institute, Van Riper gained a degree of national fame, including articles in The Washington Post and Wall Street Journal, for his role in leading the opposing "Red" enemy forces in a 2002 war game to beat U.S. Forces and send most of the 7th Fleet to the bottom of the Persian Gulf. His success was once again tied to the use of unconventional tactics, such as employing rubber boats to sink the ships and carrier pigeons for communications.

Gray developed a set of tables that tied meteorological data on moon phases with times for flares to be fired by mortars and artillery so that no portion of the area of operations was ever dark for longer than a 10-minute period. The illumination umbrella was adopted by other companies, so much so that POWs complained about the almost continual "daylight" caused by the combination of flares and moonlight.

If lights and action were part of the battalion scheme, then the "camera" was the ability to use existing technology to see and detect enemy movement passing through the southern I Corps' version of the ill-fated McNamara's Line[7] near the Demilitarized Zone separating North and South Vietnam.

Started in June 1968, the Da Nang Anti-Infiltration System was to be a 500-yard cleared barrier of concertina wire, observation towers and minefields. Never fully realized, the barrier was designed to form a semi-circle about 12,000 meters—more than seven miles—from the Da Nang Airbase, the maximum range of the rocket belt. Instead, the reality was a series of trails cut in the wire by local farmers and overgrown brush, rendering an already unworkable idea that tied up Marine resources virtually useless until 3/7 came along.

One part of the barrier was virtually intact, if underutilized. A balanced pressure seismic detection system employed buried hoses filled with liquid that could detect walking or other movement within 100 yards. The system reportedly gave false readings, but when Van Riper questioned the Marine operator and examined his log book, he learned that the readings were bunched in the hours around sunrise and sunset—about the same time one might expect infiltration.

By placing squads or fire teams to observe the areas with the highest readings, Van Riper learned that the enemy's "camouflage, concealment

---

7. The McNamara Line was a scheme launched in 1967 by Secretary of Defense Robert McNamara to build a barrier near the Demilitarized Zone between North and South Vietnam to halt enemy infiltration. It consisted of cleared areas, electronic surveillance, military fortifications and other means to make it easier to halt NVA movement. It was roundly criticized by military leaders as inefficient and resulted in tying up troops in static defense. It became a classic example of McNamara's famous hubris in applying academic solutions over the objections of leaders on the ground.

and (slow) movement was extraordinary. We had to get close to see what they were doing."

The detection system was coupled with PPS-6 ground surveillance radar sets, which were box-like apparatus mounted on tripods that enabled the operators to detect movement nearly a mile away. Add to the mix starlight scopes, clumsy and crude by today's standards of night vision equipment, and the area around Hill 10 became a brutal hunting ground for waiting Marines.

Typical was the experience of a platoon patrol base in early 1969 that detected a group of 10 NVA traced by a radar set. The patrol called a location to Mike Company headquarters, which sent a patrol to intercept the enemy, made easier when the NVA crossed a seismic line, verifying their number and direction. The result was a hasty ambush that left five NVA dead.

"We had something like 90 days with no rockets being fired out of this area where, previously, it was probably at least several times a month, if not once a week," Van Riper noted. The Meritorious Unit Commendation awarded to the battalion noted its "vigorous saturating patrols" denied the enemy the ability to effectively marshal their forces.

2
The Stage for Battle is Set

Operating astride one of the main NVA infiltration routes, the third battalion was virtually on the doorstep of the 1st Marine Division headquarters about three miles northwest on Hill 327 (Division Ridge). Throughout the war, the role of the division had been the same—the protection of Da Nang and its valuable airfield.

Likewise, the enemy's mission never wavered. Prior to the more famous battle during Tet 1968, the Communist Da Nang City Committee issued a warning order and a plan that called for the capture of the I Corps Army of the Republic of Vietnam (ARVN) Headquarters and the assault of other allied installations.

With its forces seriously depleted by the major offensive of 1968, Hanoi shifted its strategy in early 1969, moving toward carefully planned attacks on towns and bases by smaller units and sappers. Nonetheless, senior communist leaders believed that an offensive, perhaps not as ambitious as 1968, still offered the opportunity for success in the region. The Communists correctly interpreted that the will of the American people continued to wane and that a thrust at Da Nang held the potential for a major victory in the region. Marine intelligence later concluded that this was to be part of a multi-phased affair to be conducted in the 1st Division TAOR over a significant period of time.

The plan developed in late 1968 by senior officers of Group 44, military headquarters for Quang Nam Province, which included Hieu Duc, called for the 141st NVA Regiment, along with the 21st, 31st and 36th NVA regiments, and local Main Force VC units to besiege Da Nang, primarily from the west and the south.

The 141st operation would be hampered by the fact that the 2,400-man regiment had not recovered from a severe bout of malaria in 1968, which left it at half-strength. As late as mid-February 1969, Marine intelligence learned that a 500-man force of the regiment was reported to be "tired and demoralized" and in need of food and supplies., according to a special study of Charlie Ridge and surrounding areas by the 1st Marine Division.

The objective of the overly ambitious plan was to destroy 3/7 and force the 1st Marine Division to commit remaining resources to the area. NVA strategists assumed that South Vietnamese, Republic of Korea and other Marine units would have their hands full with attacks by other NVA and VC units and be unable to help.

Official resources indicate the NVA were conducting reconnaissance operations in the area shortly after 3/7 assumed its new area of responsibility. In fact, on December 13, 1968, a Kilo third platoon squad spotted a company moving west toward Charlie Ridge near Hill 41; it sprung an ambush at close range with small arms and Claymore Mines, killing five enemy.

"We learned from debriefing a POW and captured notebooks that they were a sapper (combat engineer) company which had been conducting a recon into Da Nang . . . in anticipation of a Tet offensive," John Bender noted.

In preparation for the February attack, the 36th NVA Regiment moved from its base in the Que Son Mountains through Go Noi Island, more than 10 miles southwest of Da Nang. The North Vietnamese force would threaten, with the support of the 21st NVA regiment, the 2nd Battalion 1st Marine Regiment guarding the southeastern flank below the Marble Mountain Air Facility. Part of the 141st Regiment and the 31st Regiment lay in wait in Elephant Valley northwest of Da Nang.

The lion's share of the battle fell to the remainder of the 141st Regiment, which would come from Charlie Ridge and drive east and north toward the Song Tuy Loan northeast of Hill 10 and capture the Cobb Bridge across the river. With the bridge intact, the NVA would control Route 540 and the southern approach through the Dai La pass to Hill 327.

As important as the set piece battles that would follow during the 1969 Tet offensive, it was the work of squads and fire teams since taking over the TAOR in December 1968 that really paved the way for victory on the battlefield. With that strategy in place, those small units patrolling or setting ambushes scattered and disoriented the enemy, forcing them to stand and fight. Once they were fixed, it was really over for the bruised NVA as USMC commanders assaulted and massed air, artillery and other weapons to crush the enemy.

3
NVA Off to a Rocky Start

The battalion's vigilance paid off about midnight on February 22 when a Marine monitoring the seismic intrusion system detected movement south of Mike Tower in the Da Nang barrier and alerted a squad from Mike's first platoon that was set up in the area. About an hour later, the waiting Marines sprung the ambush a mile south of Hill 10 and 2.5 miles west of the Bo Bans area where the company would be heavily engaged later that morning.

Platoon commander 2nd Lt. Lee Neely, later a lieutenant colonel, remembers that "we got eight of them, including the company commander, but I don't know how many got away." The patrol also captured the first sergeant of an 82-mm mortar company from the 141st Regiment. The POW revealed in later interrogation that the battalion command post (CP) was their main target.

Neely briefly reported the action to Van Riper on Hill 10 and was barely into his second report when 2nd Lt. Bill Donaldson broke into the radio net with emergency traffic that his patrols were detecting movement.

That same morning, rocket and mortar teams attacked the Deep Water Pier in Da Nang, damaging an A-6A fixed-wing aircraft and six helicopters; they also set fire to a 450,000-gallon fuel storage area at the airport. The 3rd Battalion, 1st Marines attacked enemy troops approaching the two Son Cau Do bridges south of the airfield, killing 47 VC and halting any attempt to control two critical highway approaches to Da Nang. The 2nd Battalion, 1st Marines repulsed an attack on its command post almost four miles south of Marble Mountain by about 70 enemy soldiers from the 3rd Sapper Battalion, supported by mortars from the 36th NVA Regiment, killing 15 VC and NVA.

Other activity that morning saw an early assault by satchel-carrying NVA who penetrated the perimeter of the 1st Marine Division CP on Hill 327 in at least two places before being driven off by a counterattack from the Headquarters Battalion Provisional Company and security forces. The 26th Marines staved off a similar incursion on the northern slope of Hill 327 and the 2nd Battalion, 7th Marines, protecting the right flank of the division headquarters, faced NVA in the perimeter wire, but beat back the attack and killed or captured 75 enemy soldiers.

At dawn on February 23, Marine units from the Da Nang Airbase forced a VC unit into a bamboo-encircled cemetery in a factory complex near the Hoa Vang District Headquarters. The next day, the 21st ARVN Ranger Battalion assaulted and killed 57 as the enemy tried to withdraw to the south and join the other fleeing units that had been sent north to directly attack Da Nang.

Near Hill 10, the squads and fire teams of Donaldson's third platoon were spread out in ambush sites about two miles east of the battalion CP in an area that became inundated with NVA. The platoon commander recalled that in the late evening of the February 22, Van Riper called him to say that intelligence reports indicated that "tonight's the night."

Early the next morning, one fire team reported seeing about 100 NVA moving north in the distance; shortly thereafter, another fire team from the third platoon noticed about 40 NVA in boats crossing a small finger lake, created by a wide part of an area stream. Donaldson, who later flew F-4s before retiring as a major, called in a fire mission as they crossed.

The lieutenant established a patrol base south of the lake on the east side of Route 540 leading north to Da Nang in one of the many Vietnamese graveyards dotting the area. He sent Sgt. William Turner and a few Marines toward a nearby village where they clashed with a couple of NVA before reaching the area of the earlier artillery strike. They found no bodies but blood and a number of bandages strewn about, attesting to the work of the 105 mm artillery rounds.

Another third platoon fire team sprung an ambush northeast of the village of Durong Lam 2, near the Song Tuy Loan, and quickly ran low on ammunition in the ensuing firefight, the triggering event for the battle that would follow.

Donaldson realized they needed help and pulled together the Marines he had on hand to link up with Lance Corporal (LCpl.) Eldon Michalec and his fire team in an ambush site near the Bo Bans, at the junction of the Tuy Loan and Yen rivers. As the lieutenant moved toward Michalec, "Sgt. Turner told me to stay out of the tree lines to the west because that's where the NVA are," he said.

The Marine's prescience would be only too true for 2nd Lt. Lou Piatt and his second platoon, soon to be fighting in that area, and would prove fortuitous for Donaldson and his Marines. Much of combat can be happenstance, an altered route, a cancelled order, miscommunication or pure luck. This would be the first such circumstance for Donaldson's platoon.

As the day broke, a grey mist swirled around the legs of the Marines as they advanced through a graveyard. "Yeah it was eerie, like something out of the movies," Donaldson would remember. The group proceeded north "with the river to my right and tree line to my left and no place for cover in between. I felt very exposed and the hairs were up on the back of my neck."

The patrol moved west toward the tree line near the village of Duong Lam 2, and approached an irrigation ditch with a small foot bridge. One of the Marines spotted grass moving in the ditch as the NVA tried to creep up on the fire team that Donaldson was attempting to reach. The Marines opened fire and moved methodically up the ditch killing five NVA in their way before linking up with the fire team.

"It must have been (an enemy) CP because they had a flag (denoting a command unit) and radio," Donaldson said. The lieutenant consolidated his group in a tree line and while checking his security noticed one NVA about 100 yards to his west. Two others joined him and the group moved along a paddy dike right into the arms of the waiting Marines, who killed all three and recovered an M-16 rifle that had been lost in 1968 when the enemy overran a Mike fire team.

4
A Deadly Melee

Capt. Van Riper had been monitoring the radio from Hill 10 and already was on the way with his command group, two tanks and the second platoon down the dirt road from the northeast corner of the low hill. As they approached the "T" intersection with asphalt Route 540, Private First Class (Pfc.) Raymond Everest, who was at the front of Corporal (Cpl.) Charles Chaussy's point squad, was surprised to see two dead Marines[8] laying on the road "like someone had placed them there." Before he could figure out if they were from Donaldson's platoon or other Marines operating in the area, two NVA scurrying across the rice paddy caught his eye.

"We were kind of surprised to see (the NVA) in the (open), just busy bopping along and some even had weapons slung over their shoulders just like they belonged there," said Sgt. Maxey Gilleland, the second platoon sergeant who later served as an undercover agent with the Tennessee Bureau of Investigation.

Everest and the other Marines opened up on the NVA. The company quickly moved north on the road, then east toward the nearby village of Duong Lam 2, about a half mile from the macadam. The NVA already were hurting and the Marines begin to encounter wounded and bandaged NVA. But the enemy still had some steam and resisted the Marines who either captured or killed the enemy, including one who was shot with a pistol by the commanding officer's radio operator.

---

8. It's unlikely the Marines were from Mike since Donaldson's platoon did not incur any KIAs during the action on February 23. The incident points to the fact that 3/7 units were spread out throughout the TAOR, as were Combined Action Platoons, which were units composed of Marines and ARVN soldiers who defended fortified villages in the area.

Lieutenant Lou Piatt and his second platoon started sweeping on-line through dried rice paddies containing grass that varied knee-to shoulder-height or taller in some areas. The line of advance was east and roughly parallel to the small finger lake where Bill Donaldson's Marines had spotted the NVA in boats earlier that morning.

The battle formation moved cautiously toward the tree line border-ing Durong Lam 2 with Chaussy's first squad on the right and Cpl. Gary Walker's second squad on the left. The company CP followed in trace and a unit from the Vietnamese National Police Field Force covered the rear.

A dozen NVA soldiers were about 100 yards away, lying in the grass and behind rice paddy dikes that crisscrossed the area. They were pos-sibly remnants of units scattered in earlier fire fights with Donaldson's platoon or other Marine units. A couple of participants speculated that the NVA were facing toward another tree line to the north, the routine route for Marines circumventing the village to patrol toward the cluster of Bo Bans villages to the northeast. If so, that may account for the fact that they were caught by surprise.

Enemy soldiers and the Marines saw each other about the same time, but it was Mike that immediately assaulted. Gilleland on the right side of the line recalls the Marines went about their business calmly.

"We knew we were going to have to sweep through them. The disci-pline was good and we started moving pretty quick, not running until we started hitting pockets of resistance," he said. Van Riper recalled, "I'd never seen anything like it. You usually don't get that close in a firefight."

LCpl. Lester Weber,[9] an M-60 machine gun squad leader attached to the second platoon, rushed ahead of the attack and came upon an NVA soldier, raking the assaulting Marines with his AK-47 automatic rifle. Weber cut him down with a burst from his M-16.

With Marines and NVA engaged at close range, Weber coolly decided not to fire his weapon and instead used the butt of his rifle to pummel a

---

9. To read Weber's incredible back story and how he came to Mike Company, see "I will make you proud" in the Addendum.

second NVA. Turning from his fallen foe, he charged another 20 yards and jumped over a dike to land on top of two startled soldiers.

Either because he had an empty clip or he was too close, Weber wrenched an AK-47 from one of the NVA and used it to bludgeon both soldiers. Weber urged his comrades forward and advanced toward a fifth soldier, when he was killed, a few days before he could have rotated home.

"You would come up on them so quick, so it was really who pulled the trigger first," noted Gilleland. For the most part, the Marines went quietly about their grim business with only grunts or the thwack of fists, boots or rifle butts on the enemy or the smattering of small arms fire to mark the intense fighting. Marines burned through ammunition and there sometimes wasn't enough time to change magazines. "You know you could have just as easily kicked them as you could have shot them," Gilleland said.

© David Bruneau

Everest encountered two NVA "squatting in the rice paddy, just sitting there with their rifles. I jumped back and I opened up on them and then popped a grenade. I didn't know why I didn't blow myself up."

Walker "came right on top of an NVA who was looking in a different direction and I didn't have a chance to swing my rifle so I started kicking him before I shot him," he said. "It was a pretty hectic, intense few minutes."

Gilleland ran into a group of three and all he had was three rounds in his rifle magazine. "I know I hit one and then the other two turned and opened up," he said, "but for some reason I wasn't hit. I was standing and they were kneeling and one of them was sitting when I hit him with the standard butt stroke."

Marines had the upper hand, but the wild melee was taking its toll.

"They were yelling for a corpsman and I couldn't see where they were," HM2 Thomas J. (Doc) Wood noted. The 2nd Platoon corpsman kept yelling "yo" and Chaussey led him to Weber, who had died from a throat wound. Reaching a critically wounded Marine, he provided mouth-to-mouth resuscitation "with the battle raging within five meters of his position," Wood's Silver Star[10] Citation read.

About 75 yards north of the action, Cpl. Jim Meyer and his third squad saw the skirmish unfold, but wasn't in any position to help. He had noticed enemy soldiers trying to move around the Marines' left flank before the assault and called Piatt, who ordered the squad leader to head them off. It was not long before Meyer and his unit were fighting for their lives, but, at first, the Marines were creating deadly havoc for the NVA.

---

10. In addition to the awards referenced, Marines in this engagement certainly received a significant number of Bronze Stars, although the exact number can't be determined because the awards are not in a readily accessible central data base. For the action that day, Van Riper submitted Doc Wood for the third Navy Cross, the nation's second highest award, but it was downgraded to a Silver Star. A total of nine other Silver Stars were recommended, four of which were posthumous. Eleven Marines were recommended for Bronze Stars and 13 for Navy Commendation Medals. In addition, Van Riper received his second Silver Star, as did Lt. Col. Quinn for his role in leading the battalion during the Tet engagement.

The squad eventually reached a slightly raised cemetery and spotted NVA carrying rifles and moving amid the village huts. The Marines dropped to the ground and "we just sat there, leaning against the small gravestones and it's like shooting ducks in a pond." Pressing his attack, Meyer and his Marines clambered over a low embankment and started collecting the rifles of the slaughtered NVA.

At that point, Piatt ordered Meyer to link up with the rest of his platoon southeast of the squad's position. Meyer's point man, LCpl. Robert Escudero, was unfamiliar with the area so the squad leader moved from behind a small hut when he ran into five NVA emerging from a "hooch" wearing uniforms with unit insignias.

"My first thought was that they were South Vietnamese and I wondered how they got ahead of us," said Meyer. "I had my rifle down by my hip when I saw the Chicom (Chinese communist) grenades on their belts. I drew at the same time one NVA fired, hitting me in the thigh."

Meyer was being helped toward the road while rest of the squad moved out to rejoin their platoon, but were halted by the devastating automatic weapons fire from the concealed NVA.

During the ensuing firefight, everyone in the squad was wounded or killed. Those who could made it back to an embankment outside the village and were pinned down for rest of the afternoon. Killed were

The Cemetery

Photo by Gary Walker

17

Pfc. Norman Harmon, LCpl. Warren (Benny) Cowley, LCpl. Leon (Freddie) Tipton, who had tried to help Meyer back to the road before rejoining the squad, and Pfc. Calvin Howell, who would never see his baby daughter.

In the clamor and chaos of battle, there is a fine line separating sanity from despair. For the untested, the distinction can be lost, as it was for a young Marine, new in-country, who became hysterical and was never able to fire a shot to support Meyer's already decimated squad.

Walker recalled that another wounded Marine was crying and screaming over and over again that "we're all going to die." It finally got on the nerves of fellow squad member Cpl. Dennis Morgan, who himself was severely wounded in the shoulder, Morgan finally had enough and told him that "if you say that one more time, I'm going to kill you myself," Walker said.

Morgan was as close to anyone in Mike Company to being a legend. When other squads or platoons were in trouble, Morgan found his way to the firefight, whether his platoon or squad was engaged in the fighting or not. Morgan was awarded a Silver Star for action on September 16, 1968, when he assaulted an enemy machine gun emplacement with grenades, killing two NVA and capturing a wounded enemy soldier by carrying him on his back to his own lines across a fire-swept field.

The corporal, who had participated in the hand-to-hand encounter, wouldn't be evacuated for several hours later. And if he had his way, he wouldn't leave at all. Van Riper said that Morgan, who had been wounded a few times before in this tour, got into an argument later in the day with one of his officers, who was calling in helicopters to take out the wounded. It didn't matter that Morgan was clearly ambulatory, he said that he had "walked into everyone of these and I'm going to walk out of this one." Van Riper recalled.

It's a tenant of war that confusion is the stepchild of combat and this battle had its share.

At one point in the afternoon, a Cobra helicopter gunship was called in—probably by someone in the Mike Company CP—but it was apparently unaware of Meyer's unit and started making a run on the pinned-down Marines. Meyer didn't have the fluorescent panel to mark his position that he usually carried in his helmet. "In fact, I didn't even have a helmet," he said. Meyer was startled to see a Marine from his rear running with a panel over his head as the Cobra fired on the cluster of Marines. The brave runner then joined the beleaguered Marines for the rest of the day.

From the air, it's hard to distinguish friend from foe and the NVA were known for getting as close to their foes as possible to make it difficult to use air or supporting arms. The rest of the second platoon were engaged a mere grenade's throw from the enemy and had the same problem. "Helicopters were coming in and started firing in our positions," noted Doc Wood. "They didn't know where we were."

Meyer remains stoic about his squad's sacrifice that day. He was told at the morning briefing before moving toward the Bo Bans area that they were going to aid a fire team from Donaldson's platoon.

"We did our job correctly and attacked them, but the price was high," said Meyer of the action that day. "You have to understand that we were hungry to get out there," he said. "If we were out there, we would want Marines coming to get us." It's something all Marines accept and is part of their vaunted *esprit de corps*.

Even though Walker lost three of his own squad in the hand-to-hand melee and the rest were wounded, he was ordered to move to the left flank to help the third squad. When Walker eventually reached Meyer's position, he found the helmetless squad leader, clutching his thigh, yelling in rage over the beating his squad had taken. Walker noticed three or four Marines dead and wounded lying in the open and Meyer appealed to him to bring the wounded to safety, despite the fact that others had tried and failed.

"I just couldn't tell somebody to go out and get them," Walker said. Shucking his cumbersome flak jacket, "I told the guys to give me some cover and I jumped out with bullets beating all around me." Walker reached one Marine who had been shot in the face. The squad leader tied a battle dressing to secure the tongue of the wounded Marine to his lower jaw to keep him from swallowing it. Walker, who weighed about 115 pounds, threw the casualty on his shoulder, stumbled and ran back to Meyer's squad where he was helped by Pfcs. Lonnie Morris and Tim Wogoman.

Walker's Silver Star Citation noted that while directly exposed to sniper fire and "with full knowledge that three other companions had been mortally wounded trying to cross the same area, he raced 35 meters across the fire-swept terrain" to bring the Marine to relative safety.

5
Mike Presses On

To the southeast, the rest of Piatt's platoon regrouped on a slightly raised graveyard where an impromptu aid station had been set up. It was late morning. The heat and humidity—not to mention the intense combat—had left the Marines exhausted. "If you were walking around, you were happy," said Wood, who noticed Van Riper to the rear scanning the objective with his field glasses while standing exposed on one of the tanks.

A few Marines questioned why the tanks weren't engaged in the battle, but Van Riper had concluded that it was too risky. "I had Donaldson's platoon (somewhere) in front of me and I wouldn't have fired to the north because of the village," Van Riper said. "I don't recall using any supporting arms that first day" because of the nature of the close engagement.

With Meyer and Walker occupied on the left flank, the assault on the village would have to be handled by the remaining Marines, primarily from Chaussy's first squad, against an enemy dug-in and well prepared. "I'm surprised we didn't lose more than we did," noted Gilleland.

LCpl. Bill Faulkenberry, who carried an M-79 grenade launcher, recalled that the Marines moved north toward a structure dubbed the boathouse, a well-known concrete religious shrine with steps and open sides where villagers sometimes stored their small vessels.

On the other side of the shrine in an open area was a ditch, perhaps used for irrigation, that ran roughly north and south and was deeper at one end than the other. The ditch was parallel to a thick hedgerow of bamboo and brush near the village infested with so-called spider holes, one-main fighting positions that are concealed in the roots of vegetation to form natural fortified positions that are hard to eliminate.

As Pfc. Louis (Billy) Underwood's fire team led his squad down a trail near the ditch, "we were trying to figure out what the hell was going on, "Everest said. "I was thinking there was just a few in there and knowing the other squad was pinned down, our plan was to get on line and blow them out.'

Underwood, two members of an M-60 machine gun crew and Everest didn't get far before "rounds were coming from everywhere. I don't remember which side they were coming from," said Everest. Taking cover in the ditch, the Marines returned fire and Underwood was credited with fearlessly moving to a more advantageous position " before he is mortally wounded by a sniper," noted his Silver Star Citation.

With his fire team leader dead and the two members of the gun team wounded, Everest burned through his ammo and Underwood's. He continued firing furiously with the M-60 gun, which became overheated and eventually, the barrel warped, "And then I started tossing grenades," he said. One grenade hit a little bamboo tree and sailed over the wide-eyed Marines with Everest, he said.

The boathouse after the battle.

Photo Gary Walker Collection

22

The platoon tried a second time to assault the village against scathing automatic weapons fire. The lieutenant ordered "those that have them to pull the pin on the grenades," Faulkenberry said. "We're going to throw them and we're all going to get up and take the tree line. As soon as we stood up, AK-47s on full auto opened up and people went down. We just sort of thought we would roll them back. It's what they teach you in basic training. You put out rounds they'll put their heads down—just like you would—and then assault. It didn't work." And those that are able, take refuge in the ditch.

"I had my hands full after Underwood dies," said Wood, who "ignored hostile rounds as he moved across the fire-swept area to treat Marine casualties," according to his Silver Star Citation. At one point, Wood was treating a Marine who had been shot in the eye, eventually dragging him along the ditch. "I don't know if I would have made it without help from LCpl. Gary Cable." It was a dangerous place to be a Navy corpsman and HM3 Eugene Garrity Jr., second platoon's other Doc, was killed trying to treat wounded Marines.

Everest found himself in the ditch with Falkenberry when he noticed a wounded Marine to his front. "He was screaming, 'Oh my God, I'm dying.' I slowly made my way to him, and I knew I was probably going to get hit. When I got my hands on him, I got two shocks with two rounds or one round going two different places."

One bullet had come in under his left shoulder and into his neck before smashing out through his mouth, taking pieces of jaw with it. "I couldn't breathe and was drowning in my own blood. I remember laying there and everything leaving me and thinking: 'Don't go into shock or you're going to die.'"

Stuffing his rifle under his right arm, Everest staggered toward the rear when he met Piatt and another Marine taking cover. Otherwise occupied, Piatt told him "to get away and try to get back," Everest said. Fighting off consciousness, the wounded Marine clutched his numb arm and eventually reaches a small body of water where he fell and went under before Falkenberry and another Marine dashed out with the rounds kicking up the water around them and pulled him out.

As Doc Wood worked on him, Everest learned that sometimes the treatment can be as dangerous as the injury. Wood and others kept pushing him down and he kept sitting up because he couldn't breathe. Gilleland, who remains Everest's close friend, finally has had enough and tells them to "leave the SOB alone. Let him die if he wants to." It was that kind of Marine tough love that bolstered Everest's spirits.

The ditch provided a certain amount of concealment, but cover was another matter and enemy snipers had no shortage of targets. Not only were there snipers in the trees, but Donaldson reported finding shell casings in a two-story building in the village. Piatt later told his fellow platoon commanders that he knew it was only a matter of time before sniper fire would take him out. "Lou said he watched the sniper go right down the line, shooting one guy and going to the next" before skipping over him and targeting another Marine, Donaldson said. Piatt surmised there was some vegetation that obscured the killer's vision.

Adding to the confusion was the fact that Vietnamese civilians had taken refuge in the same ditch. Falkenberry was lying on his stomach when he noticed an NVA on a trail from the village and killed him with his M-79, a breech-loading, shotgun-type weapon. "There were eight or 10 women and some children. They were in ditch and the muzzle blast blew off every one of their (conical) hats and they are grabbing their heads like on fire and I said, 'Lord I've killed them.'" Fortunately, for the Vietnamese, he didn't.

As Piatt's position became more untenable, he ordered a withdrawal and grabbed an M-60 machine gun to deliver suppressive fire until he exhausted the ammunition and also used a Light Anti-tank Weapon (LAW) to "assure that all casualties had been evacuated," read the officer's Navy Cross commendation.

Gilleland was separated from the rest of the platoon, but he did reach the edge of the village where he found civilians in protective bunkers near their thatched huts. He saw villagers in the ditch and Marines from Piatt's group on his left returning fire. With another Marine, Gilleland moved to flank the enemy from the right. Apparently, the NVA expected such a move and raked the advancing Marines with machine guns and sniper fire, forcing them to seek cover.

The assault left in its wake a number of wounded Marines, who Gilleland said were "bleeding out." The sergeant raced across the fire-swept field at least six times to get the wounded to safety to earn the second Navy Cross of the day. "I did my job . . . they were hurt and needed assistance. I carried some back and some others I helped walk," Gilleland[11] recalled.

Walker's squad, which was pinned down with Meyer, managed to get inside the village later in the day. What was left of the two shot-up squads had spent much of the afternoon hunkered down behind the village berm dodging snipers' bullets. "They got themselves tied up in the trees and were shooting down on us," he said.

Marine marksmanship eventually paid off and "I imagine we took out five or six," Walker said. Later, he took the remaining Marines into the outskirts of the village where they killed at close range four or five NVA hiding in fighting holes.

While Piatt's platoon clashed with the NVA, Van Riper called Donaldson over his PRC-25 radio and ordered him to assault the north side of the village to relieve the enemy pressure. Moving across open rice paddies, the Marines came under fire and a sniper wounded two. The lieutenant was getting his Marines on line for the assault under concealment of smoke grenades dropped from an observation plane when Van Riper called off the assault. Once again, Donaldson's platoon avoided getting caught up in the NVA meat grinder near the village.

Donaldson eventually rejoined his company, which had regrouped to establish a defensive perimeter around the boathouse, and then set out to relieve a small security detail guarding gear left behind during his earlier engagement.

---

11. Sgt. Gilleland did three tours in Vietnam and, in addition to the Navy Cross, he received four Purple Hearts and two Bronze Stars. Among his wounds were combat injuries from a shot-down helicopter crash and a fall in a bamboo punji pit where he was speared in the foot, thigh and stomach. In a 28-year-career as an undercover narcotics officer, he was involved in more than 3,000 drug buys and 70 "hit-man" operations. The drug war of the turbulent 70s was almost as dangerous as Vietnam and during the course of his career he survived a plane crash and a drug buy that went bad. During the altercation, four dealers opened fire and Gilleland was hit twice in the head, with one bullet traveling from his temple down his face through his eye socket into his mouth. It took eight surgeries to repair the damage.

As he neared the tree line where Piatt's platoon had been pinned down, he watched Marines move on line, firing their weapons attempting to take the same positions. The Marines were from Kilo, sent to assist Mike Company, but became bogged down under intense small arms fire, including the snipers that had plagued Mike Marines.

As the attack stalled, Pfc. Robert A. Horcajo saw a fallen Marine and went to administer aid. When a corpsman arrived to help, Horcajo "fearlessly moved to an even more exposed position" to provide covering fire, according to the Silver Star Citation the Kilo Marine received posthumously for this valorous act.

There would be no rest for the exhausted Marines in the perimeter. Van Riper recalls that NVA stragglers were clashing with Marines throughout the night as the enemy tried to flee the area. "I think they either crossed the river (Tuy Loan) or used it to move back to the west," Van Riper said.

A quieter moment at the boathouse: (L-R) Pfc. Paul Barnes, Pfc. Billy Underwood, Cpl. Gary Walker and Pfc Jerry Taylor. In the doorway is LCpl Freddie Tipton. Underwood, Taylor and Tipton were killed on the 23rd.

Photo Gary Walker Collection

On the morning of the February 24, Mike continued to push northeast toward the river clearing the remaining NVA and their positions in the thick clumps of bamboo and thick vegetation with 8-inch precision artillery and other supporting arms before heading back to Hill 10. Mike had accounted for 30 NVA KIAs (actual body count—enemy casualties may have been higher), three POWs and several weapons, but the company lost 10 Marines and numerous wounded.

6
The Battalion is Committed

It was clear to Lt. Col. Quinn that he had a fight on his hands on February 23 and he committed the rest of the battalion. Mike Company had contained the NVA in a salient in the Bo Bans area, formed by the southern and western branches of the Song Tuy Loan, in the first of three pockets of resistance.

West of Van Riper's company, the action for Lima's Jim Trenam started the previous night and before it ended, his company would be squared off with the NVA in the second pocket.

The 18-year-old private first class was carrying a radio for the acting squad leader, Cpl. Ray Cole, as they moved to an ambush site about midnight on February 22. The patrol surprised a small group of North Vietnamese filling canteens and the unit's M-60 machine gun team killed two. Not too long afterward, Trenam said they heard enemy radio chatter indicating movement toward nearby Marine units, perhaps including Mike Company, nearly four miles to the east.

As Cole's squad headed back to Hill 10 about 6:30 a.m. on February 23, they were unsettled by the preponderance of communications wire strewn on the trail, indicating that a sizeable enemy force had been in the area for some time. Cole asked fellow corporal and good friend, Jeremiah Johnson, whether he wanted to travel near the point. Johnson told the him to decide and Cole moved forward, a fatal decision for the seasoned Marine, who had taken over for the regular squad leader absent for R&R.

Cole made sure his Marines were spread out along the route of march. He had Trenam do a head count, including the three "tale-end Charlies" who were carrying long, Bangalore tubes that can be assembled and used to blow tunnels. About 2:30 p.m., the squad emerged into a clearing along western branch of the Song Tuy Long near the An Tan Ridge, about a half mile northwest of Hill 10.

"When our point man went down, I thought first it was friendly fire until I saw the NVA cooking fires," Trenam noted. He wasn't the only one who was confused. An unknown group of Marines were on the squad's left in a tree line and had been informed the squad was moving near them. Johnson is hit in his right leg and he hollered, "We're Lima Company. We're Marines."

Shot again in the thigh, Johnson was bandaged by a corpsman and then went to get help "because we thought we had been pinned down by our own men. I crawled up on the hill and there were two NVA dug in, looking at me." Johnson rolled away into a nearby ditch; for some reason the NVA didn't pursue him or the prized M-79 grenade launcher he carried. By that time, his squad leader was dead and much of the squad was out of action.

Lima's third platoon was sent to help and ran into trouble at a nearby tree line, adding to the mounting casualties needing evacuation. At least one Huey "slick" helicopter tried to set down. Two other CH-46 helicopters tried to set down, but were forced to abort as gunfire swept the hastily set-up landing zone. It was growing dark before another of the banana-shaped helicopters hovered with its "chin" light illuminating the landing zone. The NVA responded with Chicom grenades and fired their AK-47s, getting close enough at one point that "the pilots were shooting their 38s (pistols) out the window to defend themselves," Trenam said.

The impending dark also brought another problem. The Marines realized that Pfcs. John J. Stahl, Thomas M. Hiday and David E. Thaxton, all barely in-country a week, were missing. A Hughes OH-6, a light, two-man observation helicopter, discovered the bodies days later, half-buried near a bomb crater along the squad's patrol route. The Marines counted earlier by Trenam still had belts of M-60 machine gun ammo around their necks but it was pretty clear that they had been tortured.

Ed White, another second platoon Marine, was ordered later to put the men in body bags. He later said that one of the Marines had his hands tied behind his back and at least one was decapitated. "It was God-awful," White said, "I was 18 and when I went back to the hooch, I drank two six packs of warm beer."

Elements of Lima Company continued in close contact near the An Tan Ridge and bottled up a stubborn enemy determined to keep a route open for remaining NVA to escape westward into the mountains. With Mike's eventual elimination of the first pocket of resistance in the Bo Ban's on the 24th, the stage was set for the battles over the next three days to eradicate the second pocket contained by Lima.

Things quieted down for Lima as it settled in for the night. However, about 8 p.m. on February 23, an India Company squad ambush turned into a major engagement in the southern part of battalion's TAOR near the village of Lau Chau, about a mile southeast of Hill 10.

India had been engaged in a running gun battle with the North Vietnamese since the day before and cornered the enemy in well-entrenched positions. India mounted a squad-sized reaction force led by 1st Lt. Paul Darling, India's executive officer, who was wounded in the engagement. The Marines eventually pulled back to a defensive position in a mud-walled cemetery.

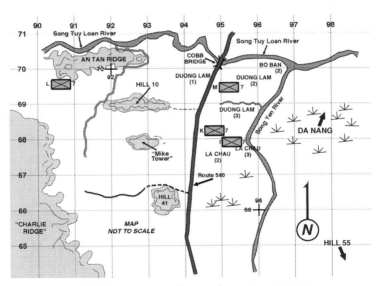

3/7 TAOR Map with coordinates and company engagements.

Map by David Bruneau

Tom Smith, a first platoon squad leader, was there and credits an on-station "Snoopy" gunship[12] with keeping the NVA at bay with its Gatling guns. The NVA were tenacious and despite the extensive use of artillery and air, they stubbornly held on while the Marines regrouped and set in for the night to bottle up the NVA in the third pocket within 3/7's area of responsibility.

The next morning, India Company's CO, 1st Lt. R.W. Ramage, and his command group joined the beleaguered Marines for a final push against the enemy, often fighting bitterly at close range. With this second group was LCpl. Edward Wolfendale who had earlier turned in his weapon and was waiting to rotate home. "Nobody ordered him to go; he just wanted to help his friends," Smith said. Attempting to reduce the enemy positions one by one, the Marines encountered an especially resilient emplacement where four wounded Marines without ammunition were pinned down in a small depression about 30 yards away.

Wolfendale rushed across what had become a killing ground with a single LAW and soon realized he could only get a shot off with the hand-held rocket launcher by exposing himself to fire. The NVA fired desperately at the kneeling Marine as he took careful aim, but before he could press the trigger, an NVA Rocket Propelled Grenade round killed him instantly. "His gallantry under fire enabled the rest of his platoon to destroy the bunker and evacuate the wounded Marines," read the Silver Star Citation presented nearly 30 years later to his mother after Smith and fellow India Marines worked to get him the recognition they felt he so justly deserved.

Lt. Col. Quinn ordered Capt. Fagan's Kilo Company to move from Hill 41, about two miles south of Hill 10 to reinforce India and to interdict the fleeing NVA. Bender's Third Platoon crossed Route 504 and set up an ambush.

---

12. The AC-47 gunship was a converted World War II DC-3, which carried three mounted 7.62 mm Gatling guns firing 6,000 rounds per minute. It was aimed by the pilot banking the side of the aircraft with the weapons side toward the target and its stream of rounds could blanket an area the size of football field in one minute. Also referred to as "Puff the Magic Dragon," named after the popular Peter, Paul and Mary song of the same name, the aircraft was often used by defenders against enemy assault, such as at Khe Sahn, and also dropped parachute flares to illuminate the battlefield.

Squad leader Joe McLenigan was one of those small unit NCOs praised by Captain Fagan for their expertise in calling for supporting arms fire. The former corporal said he noticed "a ton of movement" in the vicinity of the La Chaus and called an 11th Marine battery with a coordinate for a spotter round and then "drop 300 (meters) and fire for effect. It was right on the money."

A sweep of the area the next day found 15 NVA dead. Sweet revenge for McLenigan but small compensation for the deaths of Corpsman Larry Hartigan and LCpl. Jesse Nunez in an obscure action fought earlier near Cam Dai, just north of the Tuy Loan river.

McLenigan, who later retired as a cop in Whitemarsh Township near Philadelphia, recalls loading his squad on February 23 on trucks and heading down Route 504 with a few tanks. He didn't know where he was going, only that a group of Marines (most likely the 1st Marine Regiment) needed help. The squad joined Marines assaulting a tree line and when Nunez stopped to pick up an AK-47, he was shot. Hartigan was killed trying to provide aid. "It was the only time I lost anyone in Vietnam," McLenigan said.

With both Kilo and India Marines heavily engaged with the enemy in the vicinity of La Chau 2, the Marines made extensive use of artillery and air strikes. By the end of the day, the third pocket was reduced. It was costly for India, which lost seven Marines, including Wolfendale.

Meanwhile elements of Lima continue to press the attack on February 24 against the second pocket near An Tan Ridge, employing heavy artillery and air strikes. Lima's command group and another unit, led by the company CO, Capt. James K. Hall, reinforced the Marines. LCpl. Ray Mule's fire team was one of the units advancing against the enemy, but was held up trying to figure out the origin of a Chicom grenade pitched at his team. Aggressively pushing his company forward, Hall approached Mule's team to discover the nature of the holdup and then the captain left to locate an M-79 grenade launcher.

Returning and taking cover on the ground with the fire team, Hall asked one of the Marines: "What did you see? What direction?" and raised his head to take a look. "I heard a bunch of shots and then I heard an 'uhh' and Hall got shot right between the eyes," Mule said. The captain was on his second consecutive tour when he joined the battalion in December and was killed only a few days from rotating home.

LCpl. Harold Antonucci recalls the area near where the captain was killed as honeycombed with tunnels and anti-aircraft emplacements that were firing at helicopters and jets when they made their bombing runs.

The loss of their leader was unsettling, but there wasn't any time to mourn. Trenam said, "When Capt. Hall got killed, I remember how demoralized we were, but we had to continue (the attack)."

Terry Tirey's memories of that day are also vivid, perhaps too vivid. Tirey and his fellow Marines carried Hall to a helicopter, which was hit by a mortar round and forced down. Tiery, who was wounded, still cannot shake the "screaming and the smell of blood" from that day, causing the nightmares and the combat stress he feels today.

Capt. James Hall, left, then-CO of India, poses in January 1969 with from left, Capt. Fred Fagan, Kilo CO; 2nd Lt. Byron Weber, then-CO of Lima; Capt. Paul Van Riper, Mike CO, and the author, H&S CO.   Photo T.A. Williamson Collection

7
Eliminating the Final Pocket

The next morning on the 25th, Company L resumed the attack and although nine NVA were killed, the company could not dislodge the well-entrenched defenders and held in place for the night. Some of the heaviest fighting of the five-day period occurred at Lima's position as the company attempted flanking attacks and a frontal assault on the NVA positions near the river. Lima lost 14 Marines and its combat effectiveness was severely hampered. Lt. Col. Quinn assigned its mission to Mike and ordered Van Riper to eliminate the NVA at first light the next morning.

© David Bruneau

Trenam recalls the fighting on February 24 and 25. Lima at first had tried to sweep the An Tan ridge line toward the river. "We knew where the fire was coming from as we kept running into resistance." Closer to the river, NVA were entrenched and had at least one heavy 12.7 mm. machine gun, comparable to the U.S. 50-caliber machine gun. "We were using a lot of LAWS. Guys were bringing out (the tube-like rocket launchers) on Amtracs (amphibious tractors)."

Phil Valenzuela, attached with a machine gun team to Lima's third platoon, noted that in one of the assaults he reached a trench line while other Marines were "just tore up" attempting to flank the heavily fortified position. The Marines pulled back to let supporting arms do their work and prepared for the next assault.

"We had kind of a macabre thing," Valenzuela said. "Everybody got real quiet. We knew what was going to happen, frontal assault, and we were looking at each other, especially older guys, kind of making mental pictures in our heads of who was going to make it and who wasn't.

Cleaning out the enemy positions was a nasty, close-in business. "We used 'willy peter' (white phosphorus) grenades," Valenzuela said. "We hugged the bank right next to the river and we threw willy pete inside the holes, then threw a frag and after it went off, our gun team opened up. We were killing everything."

India and Kilo were still kicking up NVA on February 25 near the La Chaus. About 6 a.m., India Marines moving to check out a possible rocket launching site near the combat area from the 24th came under attack with heavy small arms and automatic weapons fire. After artillery and air prep, the platoon moved forward and killed four NVA and captured two prisoners.

One of the NVA was armed with a 9mm pistol and stuck in a small fighting hole under a tree. "It was either die or give up," Smith said. In spite of his tattered shorts and bandaged calf, it was clear that this NVA was somebody special. He was taller than most Vietnamese and carried himself with an arrogant demeanor, suggesting someone in authority. Attempting a ruse that he was a company commander, Nguyen That Tanh[13] finally relented during interrogation at the 1st Marine Division

---

13. For a full account of Tanh and his command, see "The Hard-Luck 141st Regiment" in the Addendum.

Headquarters that he was the CO of the 141st Regiment. It was a significant capture by the grunts of India, who got a division plaque for their trophy.

Despite the bitter fighting during the day on February 23, followed by clashes that night and the following day, Van Riper's company was relatively fresh after regrouping on Hill 10. The company was short on manpower, however, and squads like Gary Walker's were filled with newly arrived Marines.

Van Riper was wary as he pondered the intelligence reports. "This was a very prickly covered area with trees and vegetation," he said. "They were dug-in and had inflicted some pretty heavy casualties on Lima."

As he began planning, he knew that Lima had attempted to flank the enemy on the east and west, as well as a frontal assault from the south. Similar to Mike's earlier battle, the river was at the enemy's back to the north. Van Riper concluded there was no other viable option than a frontal assault. Supporting arms were not a panacea and even aircraft with 500- and 700-pound bombs had not made a dent against enemy fortifications.

The captain knew he needed to flush the NVA from their emplacements to face his Marines. The answer was CS tear gas, a commonly known riot-control agent that caused tearing and stinging to the eyes and could be virtually impossible to withstand in heavy concentrations. It had been used in Vietnam to clear tunnels and bunkers, but it was unusual to use the substance on this scale.

There were a variety of carriers to deliver the gas, but Van Riper chose as his primary weapon the portable E8 tactical CS launcher, which can be carried like a backpack. When fired together from the 16 ports on the top of the unit, the 64 35mm cartridges formed an elliptical pattern that could be adjusted to a maximum area of 150 yards from the center of the discharge.

In the early light of the 26th, Mike moved from Hill 10 northwest through the flat paddies to the southern slope of An Tan Ridge where it linked up with two platoons from Lima Company. Under prep artillery and air strikes with napalm and 500-pound "snake eye" bombs—especially effective because they deployed fins to slow the descent and place them more accurately on target—the Marines moved over the crest of the ridge without opposition.

When the company's machine guns and mortars were in place to provide supporting fire, Van Riper gave the order to don gas masks and fire the E8 launchers, sending hundreds of the cartridges through the air releasing streaming CS gas. Conditions were optimal with no wind and high humidity. In minutes, clouds of billowing gas blanketed the entire objective. Unprepared, some of the NVA soldiers bolted north toward the river where Marines on the ridge opened fire and an OV-10 Bronco, a small observation airplane, released its rockets on enemy soldiers struggling in the river.

Rushing forward, Marines panted and gasped for breath through the stifling gas masks while shooting the emerging NVA soldiers. They used

E8 Tactical CS Launcher.

CS M-79 rounds and CS hand grenades to force the more stubborn to run. Walker, who was on the ridge that day, remembers the order to don masks. "We're just like, 'oh man.' I didn't know how much more my squad could take." The gas "caught them off balance but the resistance stiffened as the gas started to dissipate," Van Riper said.

Just like Mike's first engagement on the 23rd, the area was populated with the one-man spider holes. Donaldson again was part of the action as his platoon joined other elements of Mike and two platoons from Lima to launch the attack. He recalled that the enemy could pop out anywhere. "There was a big bomb crater and (an NVA) was trying to dig himself out when (Sgt. Ronald) Jewell shot him."

Jewell continued past a hidden spider hole at the base of a tree and was "shot in the back and killed," said Donaldson, who shot the fleeing NVA while Marines were providing covering fire for Turner as he pulled Jewell back into the crater. The death of any Marine is difficult to take, but some acquire a particular poignancy.

Jewell was a popular noncommissioned officer who had been serving in an administrative position on an extended tour when he pleaded to be allowed to accompany Mike one last time before rotating home. On the first day of the attack off the An Tan Ridge, Jewell "kept asking if he could move forward," Van Riper said. "My instructions were to stay with the company command post, but he slipped off to join Donaldson."

The assault carried 100 yards through the objective before the enemy recovered and began to fight back. Marines moved slower to isolate fortified fighting positions and take them out in fire team and squad rushes supported by direct fire from tanks and a 106mm recoilless rifle mounted on an Amtrac. Half the objective was taken before the attack stalled at nightfall.

The attack resumed the morning of the 27th this time with three platoons moving from the high ground to the objective. Following an intense air and artillery bombardment, which removed almost all the remaining trees and vegetation, the lead platoon moved quickly under the CS gas and cut the objective in two to reach the river. The two trace platoons then rolled up the flanks to the east and west. For the next few days, Marines hunted down small groups of enemy soldiers, who had no clear route of escape as they aimlessly moved in the Dia La Pass-Tuy Loan Village area.

As a result of the aggressive battalion, 137 NVA were killed and nine captured. For February, Marine losses totaled 35 killed and 121 wounded—most of which, if not all, occurred in this five-day period. By mid-March, all elements of the 141st, which ceased to exist as an effective force, and 31st NVA regiments had left the 7th Marines Tactical Area of Responsibility.

During "significant contact," primarily around Da Nang, Saigon and along the Demilitarized Zone, the Communists lost 6,813 killed throughout Vietnam between February 23 and March 1, according to a Military Assistance Command monthly report for February 1969.

Unfortunately for the NVA, they would face the 3/7 Marines a month later during Operation Oklahoma Hills as the 7th Marine Regiment, along with the 51st ARVN Regiment (and later the 26th Marine Regiment), chased the NVA in the rough terrain and dense vegetation of Charlie Ridge. This time the 3/7 Marines turned the tables on the NVA by moving out in darkness and on foot so that they were on Charlie Ridge before the enemy could mount a defense. During that two-month campaign, Marines rooted out base camps serving the Ho Chi Minh Trail in Laos for the 141st and 31st regiments, relying in part on intelligence gained from Senior Captain Nguyen That Tanh, captured by India Marines on February 24.

Addendum

i. ". . . I Will Make you Proud, Sir . . ."

Who knows in what heart courage lies? There were 245 Medal of Honor recipients awarded for Viet Nam who may have known, but even the survivors now probably cannot say. If one were to ask the same question of the men who shared "C" rations with these heroes, there would be as many answers as respondents.

But with Lance Corporal Lester W. Weber, it seems obvious in retrospect where he was heading and one singular act of determination pointed the way.

Weber cast his future lot at dusk one evening in mid-January 1969 when he and two companions passed through the concertina wire of the 3/7 compound on Hill 10. Lightly armed with M-16

LCpl. Lester W. Weber

Photo taken while Weber was in boot camp at Marine Corps Recruit Depot, San Diego, CA, 1967.

USMC Photo

rifles and carrying a PRC-25 platoon radio, the men walked nonchalantly past the thatched huts and placid rice paddy lakes into a countryside that would be teeming with NVA and VC patrols after nightfall.

The patrol's departure in daylight didn't make sense to a second lieutenant standing watch in the 50-foot observation tower on top of the hill.

The officer confirmed his suspicion with the battalion Command and Control Center that no patrols were scheduled to leave then and climbed down the ladder to one of the bunkers on the perimeter defense where he ordered a corporal to follow with a hastily assembled patrol.

The sun was only a thin line on the horizon when the officer riding on the back of a commandeered ARVN motorbike saw the glow of cigarettes in a roadside pagoda. It took considerable persuasion and the added prod of the arriving patrol to convince the Marines to return to the battalion headquarters, where they excitedly poured out their story in the Headquarters and Service Company office.

Weber had served a normal 13-month tour and was on a volunteer, six-month extension that would have expired the month he was killed.

The plan Weber and the two Marines hatched was incredible. They would steal into the mountains of nearby Charlie Ridge where they would observe enemy activity along the infamous Ho Chi Minh Trail (actually a series of trails) and call for artillery strikes on the NVA troops. Once in position, they reasoned the Marine high command would have to take advantage of the opportunity. They were bored with the tedium on Hill 10 and wanted to see action with grunts in the bush.

The 20-year-old Weber's entry into the Marine Corps after high school in Hinsdale, Ill., had a problematic start. The DuPage County Sheriff arrested the diminutive Weber (5'7" and 120 pounds) for breaking into a liquor store and stealing a bottle of whiskey, according to Staff Sergeant Henry F. Walker,* who was a USMC recruiter in Downers Grove, Il.

Fortunately for Weber, the sheriff was a lieutenant colonel in the Marine Reserves and thought the 17-year-old had just gotten in with the wrong crowd. Walker said he arrived at the sheriff's office and Weber jumped up to greet the staff sergeant and asked him if he would give him "a chance to be a Marine"... I promise I will make you proud, Sir, and be the best Marine you have ever recruited."

Weber came home after boot camp in San Diego, CA wearing his dress blue uniform and the stripes of a private first class in recognition of his status as the honor graduate of his recruit training platoon. Walker was so

---

*As per entry by Henry F. Walker at http://www.dodgingbullets.info, January, 3, 2011.

impressed with Weber that he was able to get him to spend the extra 30 days leave he got for his honor status serving as his recruiting assistant.

"I'm so proud to have known this courageous Marine who truly kept his word (to be) the 'best Marine you will ever recruit,'" Walker said.

Although Weber was proud to be a Marine, not everyone in his hometown shared his view about his service. "Weber wasn't well treated at home," noted Doc Wood, who got to know the Weber when he came to Mike Company. "It was not a good time to go wandering around in uniform. I think it weighed on his mind."

At any rate, it didn't play into his resolve to join a line company.

All three Marines went before the battalion commander, who gave them fairly light punishment and transferred Weber and one of the other Marines—who went on to receive a Bronze Star—to line companies. The third was close to his normal rotation and was sent home.

ii. The Hard Luck 141st NVA Regiment

Senior Captain Nguyen That Thanh's credentials as a hardened Communist went back to the early days of the Viet Minh and their struggle against the colonial French. Shortly after the son of a schoolmaster joined the Viet Minh, Nguyen impressed his superiors with his zeal and was sent in 1950 to China for training as a military officer, returning fluent in Russian and Mandarin.

Assigned duties as an artillery officer, he took part in the epic battle at Dien Bien Phu in 1954. At some point after the Geneva peace talks, he joined the elite 141st Regiment, which was training in conventional tactics in North Vietnam. He eventually rose to the rank of executive officer and assumed command of the regiment later when the CO was incapacitated.

The saga of 141st started well for the regiment, which had been chosen to lead the final assault in northern I Corps and the anticipated victory march through Hue during Tet 1968. Ordered south in January 1968, the regiment was able to make the trip by truck within a week, unlike most units which took months to reach South Vietnam. Crossing the border with Laos, the regiment marched undetected into the A Shau Valley where they learned that Tet had not gone well and there would be no parades for Thanh's soldiers.

The regiment eventually made its way to the Ong Thu slope, west of An Hoa, Dodge City and the bitterly contested Arizona Territory. After setting up their base camp, the regiment again ran into bad luck when nearly the entire regiment came down with malaria and its estimated combat strength dropped from 2,400 to 1,600 able-bodied men. Effectiveness was further hampered by the loss of food and the regiment had to rely on supplies from the local populace and face the threat of 5th Marine Regiment patrols and ambushes.

In September 1968, the regiment was first tested when Group 44, the NVA command group for Quang Nam Province, selected it to join the assault on the Special Forces camp at Thuong Duc. The Communists briefly took the base but were beaten back with air and artillery strikes. A relief column composed primarily of 5th Marines at An Hoa eventually repulsed the attack. Up until this point, the Allies had disputed evidence of the regiment's presence in the south, but the capture of NVA prisoners left no doubt.

NVA Captured by South Vietnamese National Police and Marines near Hill 10.

Photo T.A. Williamson Collection

Partial List of Resources

Bartlett, Merrill L. "Nguyen 'Who Shall Be Victorious': An NVA Officer, 1969." *Marine Corps Gazette*, November 1989.

Fagan, Fred T., Captain USMC. "Company Commander's Notebook," *Marine Corps Gazette*, December 1970.

Murphy, Edward F. *Semper Fi Vietnam: From Da Nang to the DMZ Marine Corps Campaigns, 1965–1975.* Novato, CA: Presidio Publications, 1997.

Simmons, Edwin H. *Marines: The Illustrated History of the Vietnam War.* New York, Rufus Publications,1987.

Spector, Ronald H. *After Tet: The Bloodiest Year in Vietnam.* New York: Macmillan, 1993.

Van Riper, Paul K. Captain USMC."Riot Control Agents in Offensive Operations." *Marine Corps Gazette*, April 1972.

Vietnam Magazine. *Operation Meade River: Marine Search-and-Destroy Cordon of the Vietnam War.* Published online, June 12, 2006.

Marines in Vietnam: The Battle for Quang Nam Continues. Washington, DC: Government Printing Office, 1988.

Marines in Vietnam: Counteroffensive Operations in Southern ICTZ. Washington, DC: Government Printing Office 1997.

Marines in Vietnam: Destruction of Base Area 112. Washington, DC: Government Printing Office 1988.

Marines *in Vietnam: The Tet Offensive at Da Nang,* Washington, DC: Government Printing Office, 1997.

USMC Unit Command Chronologies. *U.S. Marine Corps in Vietnam.* The Texas Tech Virtual USMC Collection, 1968–69.